D1810272

Bold I Approach
A worship anthology for an inclusive Church

Produced by Outcome
LGBT support within the Methodist Church

ISBN: 978-1-300-92403-6

Copyright © 2013 Outcome

All rights reserved, including the right to reproduce this book, or portions thereof in any form. No part of this text may be reproduced, transmitted, downloaded, decompiled, reverse engineered, or stored, in any form or introduced into any information storage and retrieval system, in any form or by any means, whether electronic or mechanical without the express written permission of the author.

Contents

Introduction

At the end of a day-long debate the Methodist Conference passed in the same session a series of resolutions (known as 'The 1993 Resolutions'). The 6th resolution reads as follows:

Conference recognizes, affirms and celebrates the participation and ministry of lesbians and gay men in the church. Conference calls on the Methodist people to begin a pilgrimage of faith to combat repression and discrimination to work for justice and human rights and to give dignity and worth to people whatever their sexuality.

This anthology is offered to the wider church by Outcome as another step in our 20 year pilgrimage in regard to matters of sexuality.

With thanks to all those who helped make this anthology a reality.

OUTCOME

Our Aim: To build an inclusive Methodist Church

As LGBT Christians and their supporters within the Methodist Church we will:

- Challenge the Church

- Witness as LGBT Christians

- Support Church members in dealing with issues surrounding sexuality

Our Objectives:

- to support LGBT people where they are and in their Christian discipleship

- to have a lived anti homophobic policy

- to develop adherence to national legislation and human rights on sexuality and employment

- to develop and use inclusive language and style of liturgy and hymnody

- to officially recognise same sex unions

- to have greater confidence in being out.

Contact: www.outcome.co.uk

Forward

The great thing about pilgrimage is that you get to see things from different angles. I have travelled the length and breadth of Britain over the last five years and I am increasingly certain of one thing; how hard it is to see things from another person's point of view. In Shetland, London looks a very different beast than London seen from Oakwood where I live. Country and town often misunderstand each other. However, pilgrimage offers you a chance that as you travel with others and listen to them you move from where you are comfortable to other places and there review and learn respect.

I notice this of our pilgrimage. We have been mostly kind to each other and for that I am grateful and a little proud. However, we remain frustrated at the slowness of the journey since 1993. This frustration, mixed with kindness has resulted in the development of patience. For some the issues of inclusion and recognition of relationships are now more clearly matters of justice, ordinary civil justice, but also a deeply rooted sense of biblical justice. For some the challenge to throw off traditionally held views about how the Bible is authoritative and how we understand God's will must still be resisted.

I stay within the Methodist Church. I am frustrated at our slow progress, but deeply appreciative of the kindness shown to me, and I am learning patience. However, at some point the pilgrimage will conclude, and then we will discover a whole range of similar issues about sexuality, scripture, authority and the challenge of discerning God's will. We will therefore still need kindness, we will still feel frustrated, and we will still have to practise patience. For all this by God's grace, we need courage, creativity and love. So 'bold I approach' is a very good title for this anthology!

Mark Wakelin
President of Conference 2012-2013

Prayers

Uniquely and wonderfully made

Uniquely and wonderfully made by you, God, who makes all things in heaven and on earth,

Uniquely and wonderfully loved by you, God, who loves all things in heaven and on earth,

I thank you for loving me as I was, and as I am now.

I pray for those amongst my family and friends who loved me as I was, but struggle to accept me as I am.

I pray for those who have never even met me, and yet who cannot accept me as I am, an individual made in your image, an individual with a need for acceptance, for dignity, for self-esteem.

I pray for myself, for those times when the weight of prejudice and rejection threatens to overwhelm me, when despair engulfs the very heart of me, and I feel too weary to bear any more.

You have promised that you will raise up those who put their trust in you as if on eagles' wings – raise me up, so that I can fly free and unfettered, free to be who I truly am.

I bring this prayer to you, knowing I am precious and honoured in your sight, and that you love me.
Amen

Rev Janet Pybon

Act kindly, love justice and walk humbly with your God
For Pastor Charles Worley and Friends

Act kindly, love justice and walk humbly with your God.
Is this kindness when you call for us to be caged up and barred
from society,
not just ostracised and vilified, but forcefully excluded?

Is this justice when you call for our extermination,
for us to be destroyed like vermin,
an unholy holocaust of the 21st century?

Do you believe you are walking humbly with God
when you claim exclusive knowledge of his will,
arrogantly dismissing that others might also know something of
his heart and mind?

You, who place so much emphasis on God's word,
Act kindly, love justice and walk humbly with your God.

Janet Pybon

Rainbow God

Red is an angry colour
We think of those who are angry
Those who hurt others
Those who hurt themselves
And we think of the things that make us angry
All the hurts of the world
Pain & suffering
Clashes & conflict
Poverty of body & spirit

Rainbow God we pray that you will bring
unity where there is division
& wholeness wherever there is hurting

Orange reminds us of those who are excluded
As we think of the church that makes room for all
We remember those who feel they do not belong
All discriminated against because of age, colour,
religion, gender, sexuality or ability

Rainbow God we pray that you will bring
acceptance where there is disquiet
& harmony wherever there is discord

Yellow is a bright colour
We think of all those who enjoy life
We think of the people who make us feel alive
We think of our families & friends

Rainbow God we pray that you will bring
joy where there is sadness
& laughter wherever there are tears

Green makes us think of the earth

In a world ravaged by adverse weather patterns & man-made disasters
We remember those who try to make a difference
Those trying to learn the secrets of the earth
& those teaching the need to be stewards of creation

Rainbow God we pray that you will bring
respect where there is disregard
& care wherever there is indifference

Blue can be a sad colour
We think of those who are feeling blue
Those close to tears
& those overwhelmed with sadness
We think of those known to us who are ill
& all those in need of our prayers

Rainbow God we pray that you will bring
comfort where there is distress
& support wherever there is apathy

Indigo is a dark colour
We pray for all those who feel they are struggling through the night
Those who cannot see the way ahead
Those who are frightened of what tomorrow may hold

Rainbow God we pray that you will bring
light where there is darkness
& hope wherever there is fear

Violet: In church purple marks a time of waiting & preparation
We think of those awaiting test results
those on waiting lists for operations
& all suffering from terminal illnesses
We remember all those who are grieving
& those who long for release

Rainbow God we pray that you will bring
strength where there is weakness
& calm wherever there is frenzy

Rainbow God
we bring our differences before you
& ask that you will make us bright & connected
& fit for your kingdom

Amen

Rev Jan Tate

EMBRACING OUR SEXUALITY: PRAYERS OF PASSION AND PAIN

'It was you who formed my inward parts; you knit me together in my mother's womb. I praise you, for I am fearfully and wonderfully made.' (Psalm 139:13-14)

We pray with gratitude for the gift of our human sexuality. You, our generous God, have made us who we are, rich in body, mind and spirit, and with our whole humanity we offer to you our praise and our thanksgiving.

For the touch of tenderness, we thank you.

For the intimate embrace and the making of love, we thank you.

For deep and dangerous emotions, we thank you.
With joy we recognise the wonder of our creation, affirming the presence of the holy in the human, and knowing ourselves to be stamped with your image. All that we are and have comes from you, our God. May we accept with gratitude the gift of our human sexuality.

'We have not ceased praying for you and asking that you may be filled with the knowledge of God's will in all spiritual wisdom and understanding.' (Colossians 1:9)

We pray with desire for the gift of wisdom and understanding. You, our yearning God, call us to seek the narrow path that leads to life, the light that shines in the darkness, the word that brings salvation. Amidst all that is hidden and all that is revealed,

we pray for wisdom that we may interpret scripture aright;

we pray for insight to hear the cries of the human heart;

we pray for understanding as we listen to people's stories;

we pray for discernment that we may witness to all that is good and true.

Give us the guidance of your Spirit to challenge and provoke, to question and determine, to affirm and deny. From you, our God, comes the word that brings good news. May we seek with desire the gift of wisdom and understanding.

'This is my commandment, that you love one another as I have loved you. No one has greater love than this, to lay down one's life for one's friends.' (John 15:12-13)

We pray with passion for the gift of love and friendship. You, our gentle God, who came to us in Jesus to call us friends, come to us in one another that each stage of our life's journey may be enriched through sharing.

> Give us friends with whom we can be ourselves.
> Give us friends with whom we can be intimate.
> Give us friends who will tell us the truth about ourselves.
> Give us friends who will not leave us nor forsake us.

Allow us, our God, to love and to be loved, finding within the depths of our relationships a glimpse of what is holy and eternal. May we receive with passion the gift of love and friendship.

Out of the depths I cry to you, O Lord. Lord, hear my voice! Let your ears be attentive to the voice of my supplications!' (Psalm 130:1-2)

We pray with concern for the gift of peace in the midst of pain. You, our grace-filled God, know the wounds that we bear, the fears that possess us, and the regrets that haunt us. Our lives are so fragile and faithless. So we offer to you

> those who struggle with their sexuality;
> those whose experience is rejection and ridicule;
> those whose experience is grief and loneliness.

Where lives are scarred by failure, brokenness and hurt, bring your forgiveness and healing. Bring to each, our God, the assurance of your faithfulness that they may discover a renewed sense of inner worth and self-acceptance. Together may we search for the gift of peace in the midst of pain.

'There is one body and one Spirit, just as you were called to the one hope of your calling, one Lord, one faith, one baptism, one God and Father of all.' (Ephesians 4:4-6)

We pray with hope for the gift of true unity in Christ. You, our creator, redeemer and sustainer, have blessed us with difference and diversity, shaping and forming the minds and hearts of each one of us. From you we have learned to see things differently and believe things differently. Amidst all that might keep us apart, we pray that in Christ we may be one.
       Unite us to be your people, the church.
       Unite us in faithful service and witness.
       Unite us as followers of Jesus.
       Unite us in your love.
In you, our God, all barriers and divisions have been broken down, making us a new community in a new kingdom. May we hold with hope the gift of true unity in Christ.

Amen.

Graham Sparkes

SOCIALLY UNACCEPTABLE

There are many times

when
I wish my problem
would
go away.

Because its manifestation
is not
socially acceptable,
folk are always ready
to think
the wrong thing,
for prejudice
knows many subtle forms.

Then
its not only me
that gets hurt, Lord,
but
those that I love.
That
makes the hurt
even harder
to bear.

Jan Goddard

IT'S LONELY BEING DIFFERENT

It's lonely

being different, Lord.

It was a surprise
to discover
that
there were others
like myself.
I mean,
I thought that only I
was different
in this way.

Do they feel lonely,
or guilty,
or despairing, Lord?

Is there
anyone out there.....
who understands,
or cares?

Jan Goddard

AM I PREPARED ?

So,
all of a sudden, Lord,
I've decided
to tell all!
I mean
I've decided what to say
and
I shall try and pick
the right moment
to say it.

I am prepared.

But am I really prepared, Lord?
After all,
I can't control another's
reactions.
Am I prepared for disgust
or rejection?

Am I so sure that
our relationship
possesses
the love and resilience
for
such a disclosure?

I must think about that one,
Lord.

Jan Goddard

THANKS FOR THE MEMORY

I want to thank You, Lord,
for the memory of friends
who
have accepted me
as I am.
Some who share the same burden,
and some who
whilst not carrying
this burden,
are able to understand it.
Wonderful people, who probably
aren't aware of
the gift beyond price
that they have,
and which
it has been my privilege
to receive.

Thanks Lord.
Thanks for the memory!

Jan Goddard

BECAUSE OF WHAT I AM

It's strange, Lord,
but
I never thought that
I should finish up
being thankful
for
what I am.

I am thankful Lord,
because
I realise that
rather than not being able
to serve You because
of what I am,
because of what I am,
I can serve You
in
a unique way!

AMEN.

Jan Goddard

STILL HANGING IN THERE

I'm still

hanging in there, Lord,
on this great, crazy
roller-coaster
of Life.

It gets a bit
white knuckle at times
but then –
You never said
it was going
to
be easy.

Embrace me
in the protecting arms
of
Your Love,
and we'll tackle
this ride
together!

Jan Goddard

THAT I MAY BECOME WHOLE

I rise

from
Your table, Lord,
refreshed
and renewed.
Thankful
for the opportunity
for
this "other me"
to share
Your holy meal.
That
through the symbols
of
Your body…..
broken,
Your blood…..
spilt,
the both of me
might become whole
and experience
Your saving Grace,
Your redeeming power.

Jan Goddard 2000.

Liturgies

A Liturgy

Call to worship:
Love - by George Herbert

Hymn – And can it be

Prayers

And Can it be?

Dear God, like Wesley we to are left wondering at the immensity of what you did for us.

Such love and compassion for your rebellious and disobedient creation.

For some of us it's even harder to believe, because your church has tried to exclude us, lesbians, gay men, bisexuals, transgendered people and those who have dared to speak for us.

Yet we hear you speaking powerfully to us,
Calling us out of our closets and prisons of other's making.
Flooding our lives with your light.

So we step forward boldly, having nothing to fear but fear itself.

Not condemned but saved and set free by your all gracious power.

Bold now we approach the throne and receive new life and hope in Christ. Hearing the words re-echo as It can be.

To you be all praise and glory. **Amen Amen.**

Isaiah 56: 1 - 8

Joel 2: 23 – 29

Intercessions

People are invited to come forward and light a candle, whilst music plays.

We have a dream
The Methodist Conference has affirmed the joy of human sexuality as God's gift.

One day the Church will live this joy.

This is our dream
And it can be!

The church has recognised the difficulties in reflecting, thinking and speaking about sex and sexuality

One day it will be comfortable with humanity as sexual beings

This is our dream
And it can be!

Our Church has closed its doors and service books to blessing same sex relationships.

One day with open hearts and minds, it will open its doors and liturgies.

This is our dream
And it can be!

The Church has affirmed and celebrated the participation and ministry of lesbians and gay men in the church.

One day it will live as though truly meant and openly welcome all God's children irrespective of their sexuality.

This is our dream
And it can be!

The Church is on a pilgrimage of faith to combat repression and discrimination, to work for justice and human rights and to give dignity and worth to people whatever their sexuality.

This is our dream
And it can be!

We are on a pilgrimage towards the vision of the new heaven and new earth. The new Jerusalem where all find a home and a lasting memorial.

This is our dream
And it can be!

Jesus came to proclaim good news for all people, to reveal God's perfect love .   He told us to love God, to love our neighbours and to love our enemies.

This is God's vision
And it will be! Amen

Hymn I Vow to you my friends
Blessing

Eternal God, by whose power and love
you have created and redeemed us,
strengthen us in your Spirit
that we may give ourselves this day
in love to one another and to you
through Jesus Christ our Saviour.

And may the blessing of God,

Life Giver, Love Maker and Pain Bearer
Be with us all, now and forever. **Amen**

Mr Peter Smith

A LITURGY OF AFFIRMATION

(For a trans-gendered person)

Introduction   *Through the rite of infant baptism my*
given *name is John.*

In my journey through life my awareness as being a person of diverse gender developed and along with it a female persona. My own **chosen** *name for this persona is Jan to which I appended my mother's maiden name as surname. It took many years before my spiritual life was reconciled to the reality of this dual persona – that my God, knowing everything about me, still loved and cherished me. Great steps in this journey of faith have been the opportunities when in MCC Jan has been able to worship, to take communion and to be a worship leader. Throughout her journey one thing has been missing – Jan's longing to affirm her own identity and personhood before God – that was until I discovered a trans-gendered person's naming ceremony [a] on the internet, and had an opportunity to contribute to this Anthology. Here then is my liturgy of affirmation for a trans-gendered person. (For anyone who is transitioning or who has transitioned and wishes to use it, the wording may be amended to suit their own situation).*

Leader   Lord our God, the Creator and sustainer of all that is, we praise you. Life-giver and lover, we thank you for all that you have given to us and for your promise always to be with us – that there is nowhere that we can be where you are not. Lord, you know that there are times

23

when we have not been what you desire for us – our fractured lives and relationships, our un-loveliness, our forgetfulness of your presence and your sustaining love. For the times when we have tried to go it alone, we are sorry; and ask, that out of your great mercy, we may receive your forgiveness. In Jesu's name we pray.

The People   **Amen.**

Leader   Being a person of diverse gender identity is not a curse or need for shame. Rather, it is a gift. Who you are is something to be celebrated! You stand between worlds as a blessed one who, out of your blessing, blesses others simply by being your true self. [b]
We meet together in Christ's name to welcome our *brother/sister*, who is already known to God by baptism as **N** and now also wishes to be known as **M** thus affirming their full being before this community of faith.

Because God's image encompasses and transcends both male and female we are assured that we can show that image whether we present to the world as masculine or feminine. We are further assured that society need not be the arbiter of the genders with which we identify.

Brothers and sisters in Christ, **N** has come before you today, acknowledging the conflicting emotions of a trapped gender identity in their life and the

24

incongruity of their given name in the wider context of their full gender expression. In Christ there is fullness of life and for **N** that fullness includes the desire to no longer be identified exclusively as a *man/woman* but to express the wholeness of their gender identity, as a man and woman of God.

You have expressed the desire that in addition to being known by your given name, you are also recognised by your chosen name, thus affirming the wholeness of your gender identity as both a man and woman of God.

What is this chosen name?

N   **MM**

Leader

You have heard **N's** wish to be known also as **M,** a name that affirms the wholeness of **N** and **M's** being, and to be accepted in their expression of this other gender.

In Christian love I ask you therefore, to faithfully care for this your brother and sister in Christ and assist them in every way as God gives you opportunity, that they may bear witness to the faith we profess, and lead a godly life until their life's end.

Do you promise to give this support?

The People

We do.

M, we affirm you as a member of this community of faith and assure you of our continuing love.

N / M is invited to light a candle.

25

Leader	Let us pray.

Gracious God, may the light of your presence continue to strengthen **N** and **M**, so that whatever you call them to do, they may use those gender gifts with which you have blessed them to your greater glory and praise. Through Jesus Christ our Lord.

M, I affirm you as a child of God.
Go now in peace.

The People	**Amen.**

a)   Inspired by the Services of Affirmation written by Lisbeth, and Dee Ellen Dressler.
(www.susans.org).

b)   Based on 7 concepts of trans-sexuality.
(www.whosoever.org)

Jan Goddard. 2012

ANNUAL TRANSGENDER DAY OF REMEMBRANCE. 20th November

The Transgender Day of Remembrance (TDOR) is the day set aside each year when we remember those who have been killed because of hatred or fear of transgender and gender non-conforming people. Universally it is a day not only to mourn those whom we've lost but also to celebrate the lives they lived

TDOR was started to honour Rita Hester, a transgender woman who was murdered on Nov 28th 1998. TDOR continues to raise public awareness around the world of anti-transgender hate crimes and to encourage people to be allies to the transgender community. Marking this day of remembrance reminds non-transgender people that we are their sons, daughters, parents, friends and lovers.

Loving God,
out of your infinite and unconditional love
You draw all people to yourself.
We remember our trans-gendered brothers and sisters,
who have lost their lives
because of anti-transgender hatred,
violence and bigotry;
some of them
for simply being themselves,
others - because of their association
with a non gender-conforming person.

We remember too
any of your trans-gendered children
who, this moment,
are suffering the silent agonies
of shame,
of solitude.
Fearful of discovery,
ridicule, rejection or violence.

27

Loving God,
You draw **_all_** people to yourself.
Be with each we pray
enfolding them
in the arms of your unconditional, unfailing love.
Amen

Jan Goddard

Litany: New Year's Eve Party / New Year's Day Church
(Jeremiah 31:8 and Isaiah 53: 3 and 5)

The hosts:
Rachel opens the door, takes my rucksack.
Sarah on her scooter in the kitchen
washes a sieve full of rice.
I greet her with a kiss as she
washes the rice.

**See! I am going to gather them from the farthest parts of the earth,
among them the blind and the lame, a great company.
All are included, exactly as we are.**

Their home thrown open for a party,
ideal and circular, all on one floor.
They offer commitment, in a community
where commitment's hard to achieve.
They're showing it's possible,
in the face of extra odds.

**See! I am going to gather them from the farthest parts of the earth,
among them the blind and the lame, a great company.
All are included, exactly as we are.**

Rachel supports Sarah on her feet
as she jiggles in the dancing room.

28

Midnight approaches, and
stronger and stronger Sarah beats the drum.
Everyone starts clapping,
entranced by her trance.

**See! I am going to gather them from the farthest parts of the earth,
among them the blind and the lame, a great company.
All are included, exactly as we are.**

Happy New Year!
I kiss Sarah and others too.
Ana bursts into tears,
having been left by her partner of 7 ½ years.
In the midst of it all,
Rachel and Sarah.
Sarah, suffering servant, crucified one.
They're opening their home, hosting us all,
helping us bear our sorrows,
bringing us joy.

**See! I am going to gather them from the farthest parts of the earth,
among them the blind and the lame, a great company.
All are included, exactly as we are.**

Molly and David, hosts among other hosts here at church
On New Year's Day.
Before us on her scooter
Molly starts us off with notices
given crackling from shaking hands.

**See! I am going to gather them from the farthest parts of the earth,
among them the blind and the lame, a great company.
All are included, exactly as we are.**

I refer in my preaching to the vulnerability
of gays and lesbians,

and the protection of the civil partnerships law.
Last night,
they received with acceptance my news
of becoming a minister.
So you here will receive my news of
acceptance for gays and lesbians.

See! I am going to gather them from the farthest parts of the earth,
among them the blind and the lame, a great company.
All are included, exactly as we are.

Here too we drum in the New Year,
We all shake our percussive instruments
as loudly as possible to bring in the New Year.
"Impairment" Molly subtly
corrects me away from "disability"
as we drink our coffee, she with a straw,
my hands shaky after preaching.

See! I am going to gather them from the farthest parts of the earth,
among them the blind and the lame, a great company.
All are included, exactly as we are.

Molly, another suffering servant, another crucified one,
setting the tone, bidding us welcome
exactly as we are.

"He had no form or majesty that we should look at him,
nothing in his appearance that we should desire him.
But by his bruises we are healed."

Rev Francesca Rhys

Hymns and Songs

TURNING

The potter takes his piece of clay
and flings it on the spinning wheel,
and with hands skilled by years of toil
creates a vessel from the soil.
There are occasions when the piece
refuses the transforming hands
and then, once more, the clay is thrown,
but still the outcome is unknown

The Power whose voice created matter
flung out upon this spinning orb
still works his recreating skill
on those which first resist his will.
'Twas not a wheel but a simple cross
which fashioned his sublimest art,
one orb stood still, high in the sky,
to witness the Creator die.

But art born out of yearning strong
and skill honed well before earth's birth,
joined company with love, to seal
redemption from *this* potter's wheel.
The orb still turns in hands secure
the cross stands sentinel through time,
both hallmarks of a craft supreme,
a love that would each piece redeem.

Brian Thornton 1999

Celebrating Humanity

To celebrate each human birth
means striving for a better earth.
If every child has room to grow
then all of us must clearly show
how deeply they do truly care,
that all our young shall fairly share
      The wealth of humankind.

The colour of our skin, should not
dictate the nature of our lot;
how long before we understand
this planet is but one great land,
sufficient for our every need
but not so for the constant greed
      Which bedevils humankind.

Whilst half the world contented sleep
the other half can only weep.
How many children born must die?
How often must a mother's sigh
ring out in anguish and distress
to ears quite deaf to make redress
      For divisive humankind?

The young are wise in many ways,
for eyes, with age, begin to haze,
youth's vision blur, and compromise
begin to make a truth of lies.
And on these half- truths we have built
our present world, with all its guilt
      Denying humankind.

Let each of us with joy declare
and for a bright new age prepare,
when every child, wherever born,
has birthright of a brave new dawn,
where hunger, of whatever kind,

is something that is left behind
in the history of humankind.

Brian Thornton

Additional Verse for I cannot tell

I cannot tell how best to live my way of love
Within God's law and without human blame;
Nor when the Church will turn and face its history
And be the place where love dares speak its name.
But this I know, that love is from the heart of God,
And here where God has made me bodily
I learn and live the purposes of human love
And know the Saviour, Saviour of the world loves me.

Robert Evans

Made in your Image

Made in your image Lord we aim
to be, yet we deny your claim,
Of perfect love and peace within
in lives transformed and freed from sin.

Temptation draws us from your power,
to save us in this present hour
The face we show the world, denies
our Saviour's loving sacrifice.

We hide away afraid to show
the wholeness you on us bestow,
Made whole by your creative power,
we need you every passing hour.

Give us the courage to be free
to be ourselves as we should be:
Imaged on the one we serve
obedient spreaders of your Love.

O Lord forgive the masks we wear
Turn us from guilt and dark despair
Transform us by your loving grace
Until we demonstrate your face.

Rev Pat Billsborrow

Song of Exile

(owing as much to Boney M as to psalm 137)

Our songs have been sung outside the fortified citadels
for generations.
They have been crooned in gentle kisses
To our lovers,
Celebrated by smoky cabaret,
Intoned as we have wept,
Tears of fear and injustice.
We have enfolded our secrets in camps,
Erected our tents to occupy the space
Without the cathedral.
Our rainbow flags fly free,
unencumbered by air entombed in stone,
heavy with misplaced history.

What if you were to open the doors and invite us in?
Would you notice that Jesus is singing with us?
Would you be able to hear him say 'come out'?

Ms Anthea Sully

Meditations

Reflection/meditation

I have a scarf I bought in Jerusalem one time.
It has flowers, with a velvet touch, scattered along its length.
They are red and green and yellow
                 - not bright, but deep and dark –
and the petals are all outlined with golden thread.
Occasionally, randomly, one will have a single petal of
another's colour.

They are connected by the same golden thread,
travelling along the meandering black velvet stems.

         ##
####

The pilgrimage to which we committed ourselves
             20 years ago
was not the traditional pilgrimage with an
       agreed and definitive end point.

I guess we really didn't understand that when we said yes

I think some of us even had a specific route in mind
along which we would travel at good speed
to journey's end
         - but each thought a different route.

           And 20 years is
             20 YEARS ! !

But the pilgrimage is instead a

journeying alongside

It is costly and messy and painful.

It still requires attentive listening to each others' stories, even now ....

      and attentive listening to God

- the God who takes responsibility for our
      failures and mistakes
- the God who longs for us
      to love and understand
- the Jesus who may just have been impatient
      with himself rather than Philip
      when he said "Do you still not understand?"
- the God who is willing to try yet another way
      to teach us
- the God who yearns to hold us <u>all</u> as
      adult children, co-heirs with Christ
- the God who continues, lovingly, patiently,
      to journey at our speed.

###################################
#######

I have a scarf I bought in Jerusalem one time.

It spoke to me of difference and beauty
      of interlinking and mutuality
      of the joy of diversity
and our need of each other.

I saw the flowers
as   Christian, Jew, and Muslim
as   Israeli, Palestinian and Visitor
and I prayed it so
with a deep desire for justice and for peace.

Now I wonder if it offers more than that.
      Will I pray for <u>my</u> own enemy in my own pain?
      Will I allow God's golden thread

to link me with all whose different view
I completely fail to comprehend?
Will I still speak out for justice
stand up for justice
come out for justice
and yet hold out my hand in reconciling love across
dividing barriers until they fall?

Alison Tomlin

Not the Nativity

Awareness, sensations, emotions, voices, time.

Suspended, trapped between time and space. No effort is needed. I am.

In here it is dark, warm, muffled, cocooned, a twilight world that alters perception and senses. In just five short weeks there will be changes and my work will begin. But for now I float, aware and yet not fully aware. My limbs and body grow strong. Knit together so strangely. It is strange to take on human form. Being human pins you down to a particular time, a particular place. You are set irrevocably in an historical context, they think they can tie me down, put me in their box, label me, fundamentalist, mad-man, miracle worker. I know even now they will not understand, they will not grasp totally who I am. In another time and another place I was ....
Complete .... And now I float, waiting, growing, learning the task set out or me.
Knowledge of the task grows daily, even now I feel that future pain.

I hear noises.

I hear her voice, warm and smooth, she is constantly aware of my presence, and I feed on her like a parasite. I am completely dependent on this scrap of humanity for food, for oxygen, warmth, comfort. All my basic needs are met and I give nothing in return, except discomfort, extra weight and worry. I can see even now the worry that will be etched in her face when my time comes.

I swim in the warm pool, I hear its fluid motion around me. I hear a woosh as blood passes through her veins, I hear the muffled beat of her heart. I hear the women chattering as they collect their water at the well. I feel the smooth coil of cord that gives me life. I grasp, I kick, I suck, I swallow. Preparation for life they call it, those in the know, the local women who

39

prod and poke relentlessly to assure themselves that I am healthy. Is this preparation for the life I will live?

Can this really be happening to me, trapped here in this place, how can this be? What foolish plan is this that I should lie here, helpless, dependent? Who's idea was it anyway? Don't leave me here trapped inside humanity, for ever known as the mad-miracle worker. I cannot be like this. The pain of separation from that other place is too great. This plan will never work, I'll simply be another fool, another do-gooder who got what he deserved. I don't deserve this. If we are complete, as one, we don't need to go through with this plan, we can remain as always, united, perfect, aloof, we don't need humanity.

In the hot still night the woman turned restlessly, half asleep she reached out to caress the bulge in her body, but all was not well. The baby had stopped moving.

Rev Barbara Duchars

A Meditation
Luke 5v17-25

Yet it could have been any day, when people gathered together to worship God, coming as they often do from far away, but meeting like with like for comfort, for security for reassurance.

And the greater power that is present unwelcome and silences the outsider, resistant to the full demands of the Gospel.

And so-called friends may well bring those who find no way into Church, before the glaring eyes of assembled congregations in prayer. Surely, if Christ ordered the paralysed man to pick up his bed and walk, then he commands us to carry our beds around with us as part of us, not as if one love must stop before another kind of love can begin.

Cassandra Howe
'Sustaining Stories'
Outcome moving towards an inclusive Church

Heavy Loads

Jesus fell three times under the weight of the cross.
A passer-by was forced to help.

Heavy loads are hard to bear, especially when we feel alone.

What loads are you carrying?

Ask God to show you which loads you need to let go.

Imagine placing those loads at the cross of Jesus.

Let go…………….

Rev Barbara Duchars

Forgiveness

From the cross Jesus offers precious words of forgiveness to those who hurt and crucify him.
They don't know what they are doing.

Sometimes it is hard for us to forgive.

Especially when we hurt.

Especially when that hurt is so painful it feels like being crucified.

Sometimes, it seems as though people know only too well what they are doing.

Use the Jesus prayer as a way to focus on Him;

> Lord Jesus Christ (breath in)
> Son of God (breath out)
> Have mercy on me (in)
> A sinner (out)

After a while pray for a willingness to forgive those who hurt us by knowingly or unknowingly.

Rev Barbara Duchars

A letter from God

My child I love you.

I have always loved you.

I have loved you before you were born.

I know you.

I have always known you.

I know you through and through.

I know your inner fears and deepest secrets. Still I love you.

I love you. I have always loved you.

Nothing can separate you from my love.

Always. Mother and Father God.

Rev Barbara Duchars

God is not bound

God is not bound by human pride and prejudice.
God sees beyond the labels humans give.
In Christ there is neither Jew nor Greek,
male or female, straight or gay,
bisexual,
transgendered.
God looks beyond the labels and sees our individual lives
in all their fragility and vulnerability.
Hearts open to love,
hearts yearning for love,
hearts full of love to give.
God is not bound,
except by cords of love that draw us tightly to himself.
God is not bound,
except by love.
God is bound to you and to me.

Janet Pybon

And God is . . . .

And God is lesbian
and gay and God is black
and white and God is a tranny
and God is a nanny and God is a granny and God is bi and
high and great and wonderful
and God is divine and God is the vine
and God is the way and the truth and the life and God is
young and old
and God is broken by a cross and disabled by nails,
and trapped in a tomb
and homeless and refugee and rejected and despised and
God is mother and God is father and God is Jesus my brother
and Spirit my sister
and God is life in all its fullness,
and God is maker and creator, saviour and healer, judge and
jury, yesterday, today and forever.

And God is in love with me, heart, body, mind and soul: full on,
totally, physically, spiritually, intellectually, inspirationally,
friendly, passionately, tenderly, fiercely, faithfully and endlessly.

And God aches for my love, accepts it, receives, relishes it,
rejoices in it, adores it and dies for it rising with love and healing
in his wings, the love bird, the God bird, the bird of peace and
sacrifice that speaks, 'my child, my precious one, my beloved
one in whom I rejoice'

And God is maker of all things and maker of you, and me,
created in the image of the holy one, the only one, the one
and only one, the one and only holy one who made nothing in
vain and loves all that is made.

And God is and so I am and so I am for you and you for me
and thus we are who we are for each other and for God. Less
if not for, and for all thus not less and greater still if we are for
the God who is for all.

Amen

Rev Mark Wakelin

Meditation on the woman who anointed Jesus

Who do you think you are? I was raised as a Anglican. We went to church in our best clothes, took little part in the service and never argued with the vicar but I knew that I did not fit in- I'm not traditional, I like to experiment, I don't accept things at face value, I like modern songs, I'm not interested in the 'proper' way of doing things. For a long time, both there and here I was afraid to tell people what I really thought- I thought they might throw me out! Over the years that I have been here God has graciously provided me with more and more opportunities to be me! As a small example, I was afraid to raise my hands in the air, even though some times my arms almost raised themselves Are you someone who is rather proper or do you see yourself as a reckless person? What does it mean to be proper? What does it mean to be reckless? How does **what** you are shape who you are?

I invite you to read the stories about the woman who anointed Jesus

You can find them in John 12:1-3, Mark 14:3, Luke 7,36-47, and Matthew 26,6-7

Notice that we seem to have several versions of the same story: the very brief Matthew/Mark stories, and then those of John and Luke. It's unlikely, I think, that they are referring to more than one event. Which do you feel is the most accurate? Why do you think that different writers have reported the story differently? Is it because each one has emphasised the aspects which help him make the point he want to make? How do different people see you?

Mark and Matthew are much alike but the details in John's story are different, and so are those in Luke. In John's version of the story, the characters of Mary, Martha and Lazarus are named; Mary is the person who anoints Jesus' feet (not head as in the Gospel of Mark) with oil. The details of the story in John are different but the basic story is the same as in Matthew and Mark: a woman anointed Jesus' body with oil and thereby prepared him for burial. The oil was enormously costly, 300 days wages or an annual salary. Do you own anything that is worth as much as your whole income last year? Would you be willing to give that away if God asked you to?

silence

Who, exactly, do you think this woman was? The town harlot according to Luke, His dear friend Mary according to John, who seems to think that Mary does this amazing and recklessly generous act in gratitude for the raising of her brother Lazarus. Which is it? Or is it both? Is it possible that the woman featured in all four stories is the same woman and that different writers have picked up on different aspects of her character. Or that she allowed different aspects of her character to show to them? Maybe she feels safe enough with Jesus to be who she really is, the whole person.

People who are damaged in childhood, and to some extent we all are, often become very watchful. In order to keep their guard up they become vigilant and it doesn't feel safe to be themselves anywhere. I think that one of the ways in which we know we are healing is when we can find places where it is safe to be who we really are. One of the ways in which we can provide healing as a church is provide places where it is safe to be who we really are. Whichever version of this story is the most accurate, and in a sense it doesn't really matter at all, what we do know is that Jesus accepted this woman's act for what it really was, and in doing so accepted her utterly and completely. Is there somewhere where you are completely accepted for who you are? Where is it safe to be wholly you?

silence

John says that this woman wiped Jesus feet with her hair. We know even now that in some religions women are still not allowed to show their hair in public so we can perhaps imagine what a scandalous thing this was for the woman to do. Can we perhaps imagine a hint of jealousy from John, the disciple whom Jesus loved (according to John himself). I think it was an act of mothering- it was an act of intense compassion to someone that she loved and cared deeply about. Whatever Mary's intentions and reason for her action, Jesus sees it as someone caring for him when no one else has bothered . Jesus accepts the woman completely and without reservation. He accepts you in the same way. Take time now to imagine yourself in the arms and embrace of God and know that you, just as you are, that you are loved. This woman risked everything for the man she loved and He, in His turn was willing to risk pain and scandal for love of you

Silence

Prayer

Lord, Help us to know that we are loved, just as we are, whoever we are, now and always. Amen

Mrs Janet Rich

Child of my heart

The shining star of your soul fell to earth within my womb
And I nourished you

Emerging into the light, you awoke to the wide world
And I cherished you

You opened your wings, began to dance
And I rejoiced in you

You looked to me to help you fly
And I lifted you onto the wings of the wind.

What does the wide world know, that it would bind you to the earth?
Your very self shines clear to me
I will change the world to celebrate your being
And seek all my days to sustain your soul.

Eleanor Tingle July 2012

Poems

God's Love

The Lord believes in each of us.
He made us as we are,
Each an earthly angel,
Each the brightest star.

Jesus is in each of us,
Even though we may not know.
He's waiting for our welcome.
His love awaiting us... to show

Against no-one He discriminates.
Not one whom he condemns.
He adores and loves each one of us.
His love has just... no ends.

He may be God Almighty,
He may be God above,
But He longs to be our brother,
Our Father, our friend, our love.

He sent his son from Heaven,
To lead us all in love,
To free us from such slavery,
The broken, flightless dove.

Jesus gave his life for each of us,
And gave us wings of love to fly,
If the old law was word-perfect,
He would never have to die.

Because of love He rose again,

So we may know His name,
And freely are we to be beloved,
By opposite and the same.

Be we gay or straight or otherwise,
We are freed from grief and shame.
Free to be just who we are,
Accepted, confirmed, in and through His name.

Kierri Soibhan Ruth Wilson, Liberty Church Blackpool

ONE

One,
I am One,
One of those,
One of them,
A gay man, One in ten,
Mentally ill, One in four,
A Christian, One in twenty-five?
Disabled, One of how many?
On benefit, One of so many,
A fraction, of a fraction,
Divided within a fraction,
But I am One,
And I count,
And you; my friend, are One, too.

Un,
Un wyf fi,
Un o`r rheiny,
Un ohonyn nhw,
Dyn hoyw, un o bob deg,
Heb fod yn ei iawn bwyll, un o bob pedwar,
Cristion, un o bob pump ar hugain?
Yn anabl, un o dyrfa,
Ar fudd-dal, un o liaws,
Mymryn o fymryn,
Gronyn a ranwyd,
Ond Un ydywf
sy`n cyfrif,
Ac rwyt tithau, gyfaill, yn cyfrif hefyd.

Andrew J. Vinstien

GOD HATES GAYS!

God hates gays, or so they say,
It makes them quite irate,
To think that God loves anyone,
They don't define as "straight".

God hates gays, so they believe,
That's why he made Adam and Eve,
He didn't make Adam and Mike,
Or Eve and Janet, (oh no, they're dykes).

God hates gays, or so I'm told,
A question, if I may be so bold,
Gays and dykes are "ten-a-penny",
If God hates gays - why did She make so many?

Andrew J. Vinstien

BEHIND CLOSED DOORS, BEHIND CLOSED MINDS.

Behind Closed doors, behind closed minds,
The blind are busy leading the blind,
In search of something they can't find,
Not looking forward, just behind.

Behind closed doors, behind closed minds,
The rules and laws are redefined,
Building walls against this age,
Until the walls become a cage.

Behind closed doors, behind closed minds,
The blind are following the blind,
They're living always in the past,
The chains are forged, the die is cast.

Behind closed doors, behind closed minds,
The blind are still leading the blind,
Searching for the truth they left behind,
Behind closed doors, behind closed minds.

Andrew J. Vinstien

WHO?

Who are my accusers?
Who are my abusers?
Who'd insult me to my face;
Then sing about "Amazing Grace"?

Andrew J. Vinstien

DID YOU EVER?

Did you ever have a hurt so deep?
Cut up inside, just can't sleep?
Hurting, crying from deep inside?
The kind of hurt you try to hide?
Have you ever felt so small and lost?
Left all alone to pay the cost?
Betrayed by feelings, betrayed by friends?
A hurt inside that never ends?
Did you ever reach out to find love?
Did you get pushed out with a shove?
Does no-one ever seem to care?
Don't even notice you are there?

There's a little boy inside a man,
he wants to grow up if he can,
He wants to grow up straight and strong,
But everything he does seems wrong,
Getting more hurt at every turn,
In his heart the tears still burn,
Loneliness, grief, despair and fear,
Constant companions, always here,
rejected, dejected, full of doubt,
Emotions battered, must get out,
Please God, take away the pain,
Heal me, help me start again,
Show me where to make a start,
Mend again this broken heart.

Andrew J. Vinstien

HOW CRUEL WOULD GOD BE?

How cruel would God be?
If He, if She,
Created people like you and me,
With a need to love,
With a need to be loved,
Only to be denied, and condemned,
Just because we differ from the "norm".

How cruel would God be?
If She, if He,
Said it would be great to *"Love one another,
But only if you're Straight"*
How cruel would life be,
If I love you, and you love me,
But our love could never be, except platonically.

How cruel would God be?
If He, if She, if It,
Made people like you and me,
Different, yet the same,
With the same needs,
Only to be despised and rejected,
Just because we aren't *Socially acceptable*".

How cruel would God be?
If She, if He, if It, if They,
Said it was unnatural, immoral, unacceptable, a sin,
To love somebody, who like you and me,
Was made, created, in the image of God,
Straight, Gay, Lesbian, Bisexual,
All different, all the same,
How cruel would God be?

By Andrew J. Vinstien

ASYLUM

I'm a Lunatic Asylum seeker,
From over the Lunacy,
I'm another raving nut,
Growing on a Psychiatry.

My Psychoanalysister,
Says I need some therapy,
I'm a Lunatic Asylum seeker,
From over the Lunacy.

I went to see a Counsellor,
For a bit of sympathy,
But I'm still a raving nut,
Growing on a Psychiatry.

I'm a Lunatic Asylum seeker,
Who fell from a Psychiatry,
Sitting on a Prozac mountain,
With my cup of insani-tea.

A. J. Vinstien

Love the Sinner

The smiles were broad,
The handshakes were warm,
The steel of their knives was cold and hard,
As they slipped between my shoulder-blades.

Love the Sinner, Hate the Sin,
They chimed in chorus,
As their knives slipped in,
And the blood seeped out.

We aim to be inclusive here,
Willing to discriminate against everyone;
In Love, of course; all done in Love,
And the smiles broaden, and the knives twist.

Andrew J. Vinstien

All stations

We boarded together and the train halted
At every station. The family men
Were first to descend, at the green
Suburbs' invitation. The others after them.

Stepping down I show my face, but each time climb
Up once more. Politely they tell me
I'm not the sort of person they were really
Hoping for. They'd wait and see.

We'd never written or fixed up that we would
Meet each other. They'd taken fright
When their ear to the ground picked up the
Oncoming puffer. Some were straight:

'There's only one problem, the domestic
Factor we fear - (your credentials are fine).
It would not go down well with the
People round here. Try further down the line'.

You don't want my hands to help build your chapel,
You think they're impure. Now I refrain
From tearing down the church that takes me
For a saboteur. This is a plague train.

God of the side-lines, take me to a different
Destination. Lay down a track
My narrow-gauge church refuses to travel,
To new urban stations. Clickety-clack.

From 'Invitation to Pilgrimage' lesbian and gay Christian
movement Methodist Caucus.

Just because.....

Just because I am a lesbian

Doesn't mean I am unnatural

Doesn't mean I just need the right man to straighten me out

And doesn't mean I am a risk to your kids.

Just because I am a lesbian

Doesn't mean my life's a tragedy

Doesn't mean I am HIV positive

Doesn't mean I need to be healed or cured.

Just because I am a lesbian

Doesn't mean I am not a good mother

Doesn't mean I hate men or want to castrate them

Doesn't mean I don't have belief in God.

Just because I am a lesbian.

Do you know how hard it was for me to become me?

Why can't we just accept difference?

Why do you hate and fear me so much?

I am who I am – Christian, lesbian, daughter, sister, friend…

Rev Barbara Duchars

Loved

You are loved

She whispered

Deep inside

Inside my heart.

Deep in me

Where few are let in.

You are loved.

I love you.

Nothing will ever change

My love for you.

Absolutely nothing can destroy

My love for you.

Hear me deep inside

Inside your heart

That I love you.

You are loved.

Face tomorrow take

Strength for each day

Whatever may come

You are loved.

Rev Barbara Duchars

Who am I?

I'm the God with no name and I am to blame
From beginning to end, my love is the same
All have I made and nothing in vain
I set here and watch, while Creation proclaims:

I am who I am and that is my name.

We're a group with a name, albeit too tame,
Notorious, invisible, playing their game
Seeking inclusion and finding disdain
We wait and we watch for some kind of gain.

We are who we are and that is our name.

Here at the end we're still holding the blame
'You're in it for pleasure, you're in it for fame
Morals you have none. Your lifestyle's profane.'
And I stand by and watch while my partner feels pain.

I am who I am and that is my name.

Helen Garton
From Sustaining Stories

Testimony

My name is Paul, I'm 45, and I'm gay.

I grew up actually in a pretty anti-gay environment I became a Christian in my 20's and I desperately wanted to serve God, sadly, I was taught that I could change and I should fight the feelings I had.

I got married, on the day of my wedding I was in love with one of the ushers but I thought that if I got married I would change and become straight, I went through my life basically in a circle of false guilt and rejection. I couldn't understand why a loving God would condemn me to this. I wondered if he saw me as an abomination. I watched as people who "loved me" would condemn me. They just didn't know.

I fell in love with a guy next door. In the end my marriage broke down. I attempted suicide 7 times, the last time I was taken to hospital by the police.

I was outed by someone in my church. My worst nightmare came true. I would sit at the back of the church and cry (I called it the gay corner) the Vicar couldn't understand why I kept coming, I was worried what people would think of me. In truth it turned out that a lot of people in the church had already dealt with the LGBT thing and offered a lot of support.

I ended up leaving that church. Not because of the LGBT thing but because of some other things that happened and also my ex-wife went there.

Athough I'm alone now, I go to a great LGBT welcoming church, St John's Hillingdon (Anglican), they've been really supportive and have helped me an awful lot, I also found the Gay Christian Network.

Making church inclusive for people like me is really important. I still hurt, a lot. I speak to other LGBT people who simply would be to scared to enter a church. To be honest there are some church events that I don't attend because I'm worried that they might bring up the rejection again. I desperately want to serve God as I always have. I've been really encouraged by some of the different views of the gay scriptures and that actually he loves us whatever we are.

I write a blog now

you can find it here:

http://www.gcdiary.com

Another Testimony

My contact with the Methodist church has been life-long. During my later teens I became aware that I was gay. I knew this to be my real self from a very deep place within me but there were difficulties for me in fully accepting my sexuality as God's gift to me. These difficulties were magnified out of all proportion by my general observation of society's negative attitude towards homosexuals. This perception was re-affirmed at that time by my contact with people within the Methodism. At times this was a very claustrophobic place.

It was while I was existing in this place, fearful of discovery, that I felt the call of God to Local Preaching and then to the ordained Presbyteral ministry. This call was very precious to me but so was my sexuality. In following these calls I guarded myself carefully and was accredited as a Local Preacher and later accepted for training for the ministry. I well remember my feelings on arriving at theological college: 'I hope no one will discover my secret'.

This privilege of ministerial training involved not only time for study but also spiritual self-examination and development. However, for me college was also a place where prejudiced comments hurt me deeply and I felt unable to defend myself against them. Yet through all this my 'secret' was bursting to escape. While at college I joined LGCM and the Methodist Caucus. I remained very afraid of discovery and so I survived under this cloud, outwardly a content person but inwardly full of pain, confusion and a longing to be free.

This came to a focus when the Methodist Conference took the step of debating human sexuality at the 1993 Derby Conference. I attended conference with some friends and during that time I found the courage to 'come out' to them. The feeling of liberation was overwhelming; I felt like a new creation. This 'coming out' was also a spiritual exercise, not least because I had been able to 'come out' to God.

I found out that my homosexuality was not a surprise to many of my friends. It deepened our relationships rather than ruining them totally. I also discovered many people within the Methodist Church who would stand by and support me. Now, in circuit ministry, I share my whole self with people as and when I feel that I and they might be ready to hear to hear my story.

My story is not unusual. I continually give thanks that God loves me, sexuality and all. I also give thanks to God for the Methodist Church that has nurtured me in the Christian faith and which dared to discuss human sexuality and commit us to an ongoing pilgrimage.

A Methodist Minister

Resources

Books:

Courage to Love Geoffrey Duncan (Ed) DLT

Equal Rites Kittredge. Cherry and Zalmon Sherwood, editors. OUP

Quiverful. Jim Cotter. John Hunt Publishing

The Word is Out. Chris Glaser

Coming out as Sacrament. Chris Glaser. Westminster John Knox Press

The Sins of Scripture. John Shelby Spong. Harper One

Gifted by Otherness: Gay and Lesbian Christians in the Church. L.William Countryman and MR Ritle.   Moorhouse

And it Can Be. Outcome.

Living it Out. Rachel Hagger-Holt and Sarah Hagger-Holt

Prayers for an Inclusive Church Canterbury Press. ISBN978-1-85311-915-6

You Are Mine. Alison Webster. SPCK ISBN 978-0-281-05935-5

Reformation of the Heart. Chris Glaser Westminster Knox Press ISBN 0-664-22306-0

Out of the Depths Alan Weatherspoon. Church in the Market Place Publisher ISBN 978-1-899147-88-5

The Queer Bible Commentary. D. Guest, R E Goss, M West, T Bonache (eds) SCM

All Whom God has Joined. Leanne McCall Tigert and Maren Tirabassi. The Pilgrim Press

Coming out while Staying In. Leanne McCall Tigert. United Church Press

Bulletproof Faith. Candace Chellow-Hodge. Jossey-Bass

Many Members yet One Body. Craig L. Nessan. Augsburg Fortress

Dreaming of Eden. Katy Galloway (Ed) Wild Goose Publications

The Gay Gospels. Keith Sharp. Circle Books

No Ordinary Child. Jacqueline Ley. Wild Goose Publications

Coming out to God. Chris Glaser. Westminster John Knox Press

As My Own Soul. Chris Glaser. Seabury Books

Uncommon Calling. Chris Glaser. Westminster John Knox Press

We were Baptized Too. Marilyn Bennett. Alexander and James Preston. Westminster John Knox Press

Web Resources:
www. seedresources.com

www. livingitout.com

http://gaychristian.net

www.religioustolerance.org

LEFT: lesbians exploring faith together. www.left.org.uk

EFLGC: evangelical fellowship of lesbian and gay Christians. www.eflgc.org.uk

LGCM: lesbian and gay Christian movement. www.lgcm.org.uk

MCC www.mccchurch.org, info@mcchurch.net

Outer space at the Greenbelt Festival www.greenbelt.org.uk, info@greenbelt.org.uk

Songs:
All are Welcome. Marty Haugen

Close every Door. Andrew Lloyd Webber

Do you hear the People Sing? Alain Boubil and Jean-Marc Natel

I have forgiven you Jesus. Morisey

Save us All. Tracy Chapman

Freedom Song. Bob Marley

God of the Moon and Stars. Paul Field

Poetry:

Just in Case. Charlotte Mitchell

Being Human. Neil Astley. (Ed) Bloodaxe

Staying Alive. Neil Astley. (Ed) Bloodaxe
Being Alive. Neil Astley. (Ed) Bloodaxe